PB&J
USA

PB&J USA

Recipes *for* kids and adults
by kids and adults

Connie Correia Fisher

Photographs by Jacqueline M. Bellamy

Small Potatoes Press

Published by Small Potatoes Press
1106 Stokes Avenue, Collingswood, NJ 08108.

Printed in the United States of America

First edition

ISBN 0-9661200-1-9
Library of Congress Catalog Card Number: 98-96451

Attention Organizations, Schools, and Educational Facilities:
Quantity discounts are available on bulk purchases of this book for educational purposes or fundraising. Special books or book excerpts can also be created to fit specific needs. For information, please contact Small Potatoes Press, 1106 Stokes Avenue, Collingswood, NJ 08108. Call (609) 869-5207 or fax (609) 869-5247.

for

the ultimate peanut butter enthusiast, my mom,
who taught me the importance of family and how to make a mean PB&J

thank you

Jackie Bellamy for your wonderful photos and for jumping in with two feet and on a train at a moment's notice.

Bill for understanding and buying the "supplies."

Dad for loaning me Mom whenever I needed her.

Haddonfield Gourmet for going along with the wacky idea in the first place.

Steven Ridgeway for bringing the PB&J kids to Hollywood.

Barbara Fisher, Kelly Reardigan, Leigh Donadieu, Melissa Jacobs, Wendy Reisman, Tina Breslow, and Sandy Gaetano for your enthusiam, contacts, and help in getting the word out.

contents

Pictured left: Kevin Meeker of Philadelphia Fish & Company and his son Nolan.

PB&J Forever

Good friends of mine own a fantastic shop called Haddonfield Gourmet in Haddonfield, New Jersey. Bursting with thousands of imported oils and vinegars, spices and seasonings, coffees and teas, sweet confections and gourmet baskets, it is a foodie mecca. So when they hired me to do some public relations work for the shop, they were a little taken aback by my idea to sponsor a fund-raising event — a peanut butter and jelly contest for kids. "C'mon," I coaxed, "it'll be cute." "And besides," I said, "I know PB&J." Although "cute" is not a word normally associated with this upscale specialty food store or its owners, they went along with the idea anyway.

Fast forward to a hectic two months later . . . "Cute" kids, sticky and excited, gather at Haddonfield Gourmet and create PB&J masterpieces while proud parents cheer and the press take photos, shoot film, and interview the winners. The contest is a success, and as we clean up, I think, "I know PB&J, and this would make a *great* cookbook." But after trying half the night to remove a glob of peanut butter from my hair, I quickly abandon the project.

Fast forward to a not-so-busy month later . . . I have long forgotten about the PB&J cookbook idea and am at work on a new project. The phone rings, and a nice man from "The Tonight Show" says he's heard about the contest, and he thinks the idea is "cute." Could we recreate it in a month or so? Could some of the PB&J kids make their special sandwiches for Jay Leno? Could they? I answer "Yes." Boy, do I know PB&J!

Fast forward to two weeks later . . . Having frantically gathered recipes from kids and adults around the country, I have learned that there are countless ways to make a great peanut butter and jelly sandwich. Each kid has a "secret" ingredient; each adult, a guilty pleasure. There are combinations of candy and cashews, bacon and bananas: recipes and recommendations for creative concoctions. And I — ever mindful of my responsibility to the reader — have personally taste tested thousands (OK, at least 50) of them.

And PB&J isn't limited to just sandwiches. All the chefs we talked to — "Would you like to submit a peanut butter and jelly recipe for a new cookbook?" — laughed a little at first, but their PB&J-inspired gourmet recipes have raised the bar high above the basic brown bag. Petal Butter and Jelly from The Herbfarm; Peanut Butter and Jelly "Sushi" Style from Nobu; Hazelnut-Peanut Butter and Strawberry Fritters from The Rainbow Room's executive chef Waldy Malouf and his daughter Merrill — these are the things of which PB&J dreams are made.

Fast forward to today . . . It's Independence Day and as I sit listening to distant fireworks, I can see the light at the end of the tunnel — the bottom of the peanut butter jar. And I have discovered that I know nothing about PB&J. I actually live in the dark ages of PB&J where the bread is white, the jelly is grape, and the process is as simplistic as it gets: spread on jelly; spread on peanut butter; close sandwich; eat.

And I've learned that peanut butter and jelly sandwiches aren't just "cute." They're downright American.

Concord grapes (the most commonly used for grape jelly) still grow in Concord and Lexington, towns whose battles mark the start of the American Revolution. Civil War soldiers dined on "peanut porridge." A St. Louis, Missouri, physician developed peanut butter in 1890, and C.H. Sumner introduced it to the world at the Universal Exposition of 1904 in St. Louis. Historically, PB&J's first made their appearance on the ration menus in World War II. Returning GI's created an instant demand for the sandwich, and it soon became an American staple. Always the innovator, Elvis brought his favorite sandwich — fried peanut butter and banana — to the forefront of pop culture. (And Elvis is about as American as you can get.)

Dare I say, it is one of our country's greatest culinary creations. After all, what is the tried and true favorite in every American lunch box or school cafeteria? What can be made so economically, quickly, and travel so well?

Think about it on personal terms. How many of you were raised on PB&J's? (Raise your hand.) Who taught you how to make one? (Probably your mom or dad, right?) Peanut butter and jelly sandwiches not only bring back the nostalgia of childhood but, amazingly, still taste just as good today.

What food is memorable and not just because it sticks to the roof of your mouth? More importantly, what food is open to such creative interpretation, such individualistic evolution? I gotta say it's the PB&J.

Connie Correia Fisher
Collingswood, New Jersey
July 4, 1998

How To Make A
Peanut Butter And Jelly Sandwich

To make a peanut butter and jelly sandwich you need the following items: a bag of bread, a jar of peanut butter, a jar of jelly, a plate, a cutting board, a knife, and a spoon if you really want one.

Open the bag of bread. Take out two pieces of bread. Lay the two pieces of bread on the cutting board, one beside the other. Open the peanut butter jar and the jelly jar. Dip the knife into the peanut butter jar. Pull out a big gooey glob of sticky peanut butter. Don't get too much, it will make your sandwich really sticky. Smear the glob of peanut butter on one side of one of the pieces of bread. Make sure you cover the whole side of that piece of bread. Wipe the excess peanut butter that is still on the knife off on the other piece of bread. (This is so you do not get peanut butter in the jelly.)

Now, do the same thing with the jelly and the second piece of bread. Dip the knife into the jelly and try to get a glob of jelly. This is some-times difficult so you might have to use the spoon to get your glob of jelly. Once you have the glob of jelly, spread it on your second piece of bread. Be careful, the jelly sometimes tends to slip and slide off bread, so try not to make a mess.

Then you take the piece of bread with the peanut butter on it and the piece of bread with the jelly on it and put them together. When you put the pieces of bread together, make sure that the sides that have either peanut butter or jelly are the sides that are touching.

Lay the sandwich back onto the cutting board. Using the knife, cut the sandwich in any way you want. You don't even have to cut the sandwich if you don't want to. After you have cut the sandwich, put the pieces on the plate.

Close the jars and the bread bag and put them away. Put the cutting board and the knife and the spoon in the dishwasher. Finally, take the plate to where you want to eat and sit down and eat it. Enjoy.

Rachel, age 13
Kennett Square, Pennsylvania.
This was written when she was in sixth grade.

Classic
PB&J

Pictured left: Tracy and Amy Nieporent of Montrachet and their sons Matt and Robby.

PB&J Rollups

1 piece of bread (any kind will do)
1 teaspoon peanut butter
1 teaspoon jelly or jam

Place bread onto a cutting board or flat surface. Using a rolling pin, roll the bread out until it is flat. Spread peanut butter over flat bread surface; then add jelly. Slowly roll the bread from the bottom up, making a swirl in the bread. Eat or place a toothpick in bread to hold in place until you are ready to eat.

Serves 1

Marianne, age 32
Preschool Teacher
Rochester, New York
http://members.aol.com/Sgrmagnlia/cooking.html

Industrial PB&J

2 pieces challah bread
peanut butter
raspberry jelly

On challah bread, spread peanut butter and jelly and make a sandwich. Wrap in tin foil. Then iron it with a regular iron until it's hot and flat. MMMM. Yum!

Edward L. Feldman - Furniture Guy, age baby boomer
Star of the Learning Channel's "Furniture To Go" and "Men in Toolbelts"
Philadelphia, Pennsylvania

Grilled PB&J

Spread peanut butter and jelly on 2 slices of potato bread. (Don't over load the sandwich or spread PB&J too close to the edges, or the sandwich will leak.) Put the slices together in the usual way. Melt butter in a fry pan and grill sandwich until golden and crisp.

Cheri, age 31
Historic Tour Guide by Horse Drawn Carriage
Philadelphia, Pennsylvania

Isaiah's Double Decker

3 pieces of white bread
marshmallow spread
creamy peanut butter
grape jelly
cream cheese, soft

Put 3 pieces of bread down. Put marshmallow topping and peanut butter on 1 piece. Put jelly on 1 piece; put cream cheese on the last piece. Stack them up.

Isaiah, age 7
Haddonfield, New Jersey

WINNER! The Kid's Ultimate Peanut Butter and Jelly Contest.

As seen on The Tonight Show with Jay Leno

Nutter Butter Sandwich

We enjoyed this favorite as kids — when Mom wasn't watching.

2 slices of bread
peanut butter
marshmallow spread

Spread one piece of bread liberally with peanut butter. Coat the other with marshmallow spread. Slap together and eat.

P.S. Make sure you have something to drink nearby!

Mary, age 43
President, BookZone.com
Phoenix, Arizona

(**Note:** When packing the above sandwich in a lunch, you just put a glob of marshmallow topping in the middle of one slice and put the slices together. The marshmallow will spread out by itself by lunch time.)

Meghan, age 9
Cherry Hill, New Jersey

Peanut Butter & Banana Sandwich

Spread both sides of your favorite bread with peanut butter. Cut a banana in quarters — 4 parts (after you take the skin off, of course). Place the 4 slices of banana in the bread on the peanut butter side, cut in half, and EAT, EAT, EAT!!

Samantha, age 8
Detroit, Michigan

The Elvis: Fried Peanut Butter Banana

1 ripe banana
2 slices white bread, lightly toasted
peanut butter
butter

Mash the banana with a fork. Spread the peanut butter on 1 piece of toast and the mashed banana on the other. Heat butter in a nonstick pan and fry the sandwich until each side is crispy and golden. Eat while it's hot. Oooohh, baby.

Joel, age 23
Physical Therapy Graduate Student
Greenville, North Carolina

Banana and Bologna

2 slices wheat bread, toasted
chunky peanut butter
raspberry or strawberry jam
1/2 banana, thinly sliced
1 slice bologna

Spread peanut butter and jam on both slices. Place banana on top of one peanut butter/jam slice. Top with bologna. Cover with other slice. Cut in half and serve.

**Gerard Brunett, age 36
Executive Chef, Stein Eriksen Lodge
Park City, Utah**

The Lunker

Pretty simple, really. Sour dough bread, peanut butter, strawberry jelly, banana, and mayo. It's yummy.

**Tom, age 58
Owner, Tutor and Spunk's Deli
Dana Point, California**

Bananza Sandwich

2 slices of bread
peanut butter
marshmallow spread
banana slices
raisins

Spread peanut butter and marshmallow topping on bread. Place bananas on bread and sprinkle with raisins. Put bread together and eat it!

Jake, age 11
Cherry Hill, New Jersey

Nuts & Honey

Spread peanut butter on two slices of apotato bread. Spoon some honey onto 1 slice. Cut a banana into circles and put some on top of honey. Sprinkle on some chopped walnuts.

Michael, age 7
Cherry Hill, New Jersey

Nancy's Halloween Special

2 slices raisin bread
2 tablespoons peanut butter
1/2 banana, sliced
1 piece green leaf lettuce
1 tablespoon salad dressing spread

Spread peanut butter on each slice. Place sliced banana on peanut butter. Spread salad dressing spread on banana. Put lettuce in middle and put together. No need to slice; just dig in. When finished, treat yourself to a piece of Halloween candy.

Nancy, age 39+
Mom of Dan Dogan, Executive Chef of Terrace at Greenhill
Wilmington, Delaware

Peanut Butter Surprise

You can make several of these easy sandwiches at a time and freeze the extras for up to a month. Then you will always have an extra sandwich made if you're squeezed for time.

6 slices sandwich bread, white or wheat
1/4 cup chunky peanut butter
2 tablespoons orange juice
1/4 cup raisins

Lay out bread slices. In small bowl, combine peanut butter and orange juice. Stir well. Add raisins. Spread filling between bread slices.

Sandra K. Nissenberg MS, RD, and Barbara N. Pearl, MS, RD
Authors of *Brown Bag Success*
Buffalo Grove, Illinois

Broiled Sugar Apple Sandwich

rye bread, lightly toasted
peanut butter
apple slices
butter
cinnamon
sugar

Spread peanut butter on bread; cover with apple slices. Top with a few, thin pats of butter. Sprinkle on cinnamon and sugar. Broil in toaster oven until butter melts and sugar starts to caramelize.

Susan, age 28
Stay-at-home Mom
Kirkland, Washington

Walnut Butter and Apricot Jam Sandwiches

1 cups walnut pieces (about 6 ounces)
1/2 teaspoon brown sugar
pinch of salt
1/4 cup apricot jam (or other jam)
8 slices whole wheat bread

Place walnuts, brown sugar, and salt in the work bowl of a food processor. Process until a smooth paste forms, scraping down the sides of the bowl once or twice as necessary.

Spread the walnut butter on 4 slices of bread. Spread the jam on the remaining 4 slices. Cover the walnut butter slices with the jam slices to make the sandwiches.

Makes 4 sandwiches

Lauren Chattman
Author of *Cool Kitchen*
Sag Harbor, New York

Reprinted with permission. © Lauren Chattman, COOL KITCHEN,
William Morrow and Company, Inc., 1998.

Cashew Butter & Chips

cashew butter
2 slices challah bread
mini chocolate chips

Spread cashew butter on two slices of challah. Sprinkle chips over the cashew butter. Close sandwich face to face. Cut in half and gobble it up!

Erica, age 9
Voorhees, New Jersey

Chips & Cherry Sandwich

2 slices white bread (I like Great Harvest Farmhouse White)
chunky reduced fat peanut butter
cherry preserves
mini chocolate chips

Toast bread lightly. Spread 1 slice with peanut butter. Spread 1 slice with cherry preserves. Sprinkle preserve side with mini chocolate chips. Put slices together. Cut in half and share with a friend.

Elizabeth, age 10
Cherry Hill, NJ

FINALIST! The Kid's Ultimate Peanut Butter and Jelly Contest.

Edible Menorah

1 slice bread
peanut butter
small, thin pretzel sticks
raisins or chocolate chips

Spread peanut butter on the bread. Position pretzel sticks as candles on the Menorah (crossbar at bottom, 4 sticks on each side, middle stick slightly raised). Use a raisin or chocolate chip as a flame at top of each stick. When complete, each child gets to eat his/her Menorah. Enjoy.

Serves 1

Felicia, over 30 but still thinking like a kid
Director of Temple Beth Sholom Nursery School and Kindergarten
Fair Lawn, New Jersey

Beyond White Bread and Grape Jelly

Pictured left: Matt and Robby Nieporent of Tribeca Bakery.

Philly PB&J

Spread cream cheese on 1 side of hoagie roll. Spread crunchy peanut butter on cream cheese. Top with chocolate kisses. Spread strawberry jelly on other half.

Francis, age 9
Philadelphia, Pennsylvania

FINALIST! The Kid's Ultimate Peanut Butter and Jelly Contest.

Peanut Butter Banana Dogs

8 hot dog buns, split
2 tablespoons butter or margarine, softened
1/2 cup chunky peanut butter
1 teaspoon ground cinnamon
2 tablespoons honey
3 to 4 medium bananas, sliced

Spread cut sides of hot dog buns with softened butter. Broil 6 inches from heat (with electric oven door partially open) for 1 to 2 minutes or until lightly toasted. Stir together peanut butter, cinnamon, and honey; spread evenly over toasted side of hot dog buns. Top with banana slices.

Banana Bread "Tea Sandwich" with Pineapple Jam and Chocolate Covered Macadamia Peanut Butter

Once known as the pineapple island for its 20,000 acres of pineapples that were harvested and shipped around the world, the tiny island of Lanai in Hawaii is now home to two luxurious resorts and still raises a small crop of sweet "sugar" pineapples for the local populace.

8 ounces chocolate covered macadamia nuts
3 ounces peanut butter
12 slices banana bread
3 ounces pineapple jam

Lightly crush macadamia nuts in food processor. Place in small bowl and mix well with peanut butter. Mixture should be course but easy to spread. Spread 6 slices of bread with macadamia nut butter and then cover generously with pineapple jam. Place remaining banana bread on top and serve. Makes 6 sandwiches.

David Britton
Executive Chef, The Manele Bay Hotel
Lanai, Hawaii

Banana Bread PB&J

2 slices banana bread
creamy peanut butter
raspberry jelly
thin, crunchy pretzels

Take banana bread pieces and lay them on a plate. Spread peanut butter on 1 piece and raspberry jelly on the other. Stick pretzels in the peanut butter and stick the bread pieces together.

Bite. Yum good!

Laura, age 10
Pillesgrove, New Jersey

Winner! The Kid's Ultimate Peanut Butter and Jelly Contest.

Hana PB&J

2 slices Hana banana bread
1 tablespoon homemade peanut butter
1 tablespoon Hawaiian guava jelly
1 banana, sliced
1/2 teaspoon powered sugar

Spread the peanut butter on one slice and spread the jelly on the other slice. Place sliced banana on either slice. Close and sprinkle the powdered sugar on both sides.

Danny Baker, age 36
Chef, Hana-Maui Hotel
Maui, Hawaii

Petal Butter and Jelly

6 tablespoons hazelnut butter
2 tablespoons lavender honey
4 slices banana bread
6 tablespoons rose petal jelly
a mixture of petals from old-fashioned roses, calendula, or tuberose begonias
  and johnny jump up, violet, or borage blossoms.

Stir the hazelnut butter and honey together and spread it on the slices of
banana bread. Top with rose petal jelly. Sprinkle with the flowers.

Makes 4 open-faced sandwiches

Jerry Traunfeld, age 38
Chef, The Herbfarm and Author of the upcoming *The Herbfarm Cookbook*
Fall City, Washington

Bear Kingdom's Jelly Sandwich

Mix equal parts of "smooth" peanut butter and homemade or Bear Kingdom Muscadine* jelly together. (This stops the inevitable "squishing out of the jelly" that occurs when you take a bite of PB&J.) Spread peanut butter and jelly mixture on wheat bread. Enjoy! *Muscadines are a grape-like fruit of the southern U.S. — a delightful change from the common grape flavor!

Dennis Kolb, age 55
Chef/President, Bear Kingdom Vineyard, Inc.
Little Rock, Arkansas
www.bbonline.com/vnd/bearkingdom

Muscadine Jelly

2 quarts muscadine or fruit of your choice
water to cover
1.75 ounces pectin
7 cups sugar

Wash and stem fruit. Cover with water and simmer until hulls are tender. Extract 5 cups juice using a colander or fruit press. (Regardless of the amount of fresh fruit you start with, you need at least 5 cups of juice to make one batch of jelly.) Add pectin. Bring to rolling boil. Quickly add sugar and return to rolling boil for 1 minute. Remove from heat. Remove foam, pour and seal. Yields 4 pints.

Super Crunch Peanut Butter and Jelly Bagel

8 tablespoons chunky peanut butter
3 tablespoons dried cherries
2 tablespoons mini chocolate chips
6 tablespoons cherry or blueberry preserves
3 tablespoons water
4 plain bagels, toasted

In a small bowl, combine peanut butter, dried cherries, and chocolate chips; set aside. Put preserves and water in a blender and puree until smooth. Pour into a squirt bottle.

   Spread peanut butter mixture on each bagel half and then squirt preserves on each side in a zigzag design or put squirt bottle on table and let kids have fun with their own designs.

Serves 4

Trish Morrissey, age 28
Executive Chef, Philadelphia Fish & Company
Philadelphia, Pennsylvania

Blueberry Crunch Sandwich

3 blueberry bagels, split
peanut butter
honey
peanuts
chocolate chips

Spread peanut butter on 3 bagel pieces. Spread some honey on top of that. Sprinkle on peanuts and chocolate chips. Put some peanut butter on the other bagel pieces and put them on top to make a sandwich.

   (I make 3 sandwiches so that I can eat one, and I can share with my sister Alyssa and my friend Donny. You can make as many as you need to.)

Joshua, age 7
Jacksonville, Florida

PB Wheels

flour tortilla
peanut butter
marshmallow spread
golden raisins

Spread peanut butter and then marshmallow spread on tortilla. Sprinkle on raisins. Roll up and slice into rounds.

Ann-Michelle, age 31
Speech-Language Pathologist
Philadelphia, Pennsylvania

Shop Rite Wrap

This recipe calls for flour tortillas. I prefer apple, whole wheat, or cinnamon.

1/4 cup peanut butter
2 10" tortillas, flour (any flavor except herb)
1½ cup sliced bananas
3/4 cup granola
1/4 cup raisins or any dried fruit
1/4 cup yogurt, any flavor
2 teaspoon honey

Divide peanut butter and spread evenly over tortillas, leaving a 1-inch border around edge. Combine remaining ingredients in a small bowl. Divide evenly between the 2 tortillas. Roll and enjoy!

Serves 2

Ron Ravitz, age 44,
Owner, Shop Rite Stores
Cherry Hill, New Jersey

Peanut Butter and Jelly Rollups

flour tortilla
peanut butter, any kind
grape jelly
multicolored sprinkles (optional)

Spread tortilla with peanut butter; then with jelly. Sprinkle lightly with sprinkles. Roll it up and eat.

Julia, age 8
Goleta, California

Hot Southwestern Style PB&J

Take a big tortilla, put it in the microwave for 20 seconds. Spread peanut butter all over it and watch it melt nicely. Take some jelly and drop it here and there on the tortilla. Roll it up and eat it.

Benjamin, age 10
Raleigh, North Carolina

Afternoon Snack Waffle

I eat this when I'm still hungry from lunch.

Toast a frozen blueberry waffle. Spread creamy peanut butter on hot waffle so that the peanut butter melts. (If it doesn't melt enough, stick it back in the warm toaster oven.) Sprinkle with cinnamon and sugar.

Elizabeth, age 9
Minneapolis, Minnesota

Peanut Butter Cracker Stackers

Use you favorite crackers. Spread peanut butter on the cracker. Spoon a small amount of jelly on top of the peanut butter. Take a whole piece of American cheese and fold it in half twice. Then break it apart on the fold into 4 quarters. Place one quarter of the cheese on top of the jelly. Put another cracker on top of the cheese. Eat it over a plate because the jelly squirts sometimes.

Meghan, age 9
Cherry Hill, New Jersey

Savory
Sandwiches
and Snacks

Pictured left: Michael McNally of London Grill and his son Jake.

Grilled Shrimp with Thai Peanut Butter Spread & Apricot Marmalade

1 pound medium shrimp
3 tablespoons olive oil
salt and pepper to season
4 6-inch tortillas
Thai Peanut Spread (see recipe)
Apricot Marmalade Glaze (see recipe)

Toss shrimp with 2 tablespoons oil and salt and pepper. Grill 2 to 3 minutes on each side. Lightly rub tortilla with remaining oil. Place on grill 30 seconds on each side. Spread with Thai peanut spread. Lay 5 or 6 shrimp on tortillas. Place a tablespoon of glaze on shrimp. Roll up and serve.

Serves 4

Michael McNally, age 42
Chef/Owner, London Grill
Philadelphia, Pennsylvania

Thai Peanut Spread

1-inch piece of fresh ginger, chopped

3 cloves garlic, chopped

1 teaspoon curry paste

1 cup chunky peanut butter

3 tablespoons sugar

3 teaspoons Thai fish sauce

3/4 cup coconut milk

Combine all ingredients in food processor and process until smooth.

Apricot Marmalade Glaze

1 cup apricot marmalade

1 cup cider vinegar

1/2 teaspoon black pepper

1 star anise

1/2 teaspoon ground coriander

2 teaspoons minced ginger

2 tablespoons chopped cilantro

Combine all ingredients in saucepan; bring to a boil. Simmer until syrupy and strain.

Simple Sandwich

mayonnaise
cucumber, peeled and sliced
egg, boiled and sliced
peanut butter
2 slices white bread
pieces of any cooked fish
pieces of cooked chicken

Put mayonnaise over the cucumber and egg and spread peanut butter over each piece of bread. Sandwich the cucumber and egg with small pieces of fish and sandwich the whole thing with pieces of chicken and finally the bread.

Ho Cheeng Tse, age 14
Singapore

Oyster Open-Faced

Spread peanut butter on toasted whole wheat bread. Top with smoked oysters and serve open-faced.

Judy Faye
Executive Producer of the Food Network's The Book and the Cook
Philadelphia, Pennsylvania

Fish on Bagel

onion bagel
peanut butter
salsa
little fish-shaped crackers

Slice and toast bagel. Spread both sides with the peanut butter; then with the salsa. Let the fish "swim" in the salsa.

Eddie, age 11
Wilmington, Delaware

Pregnant Wife Sandwich

My wife ate this when she was pregnant. But only once.

Toasted rye bread topped with peanut butter, grape jelly, bread and butter pickles, and potato chips.

David, age 27
Sales Representative
Ames, Iowa

Purple Bull

Go figure — I ate this as a kid. Ok, I called it a purple bull. It's peanut butter, butter, a big slice of red onion (ergo purple bull), and a slice of salami. The sandwich was made with just white bread; once in a while on a kaiser roll.

Mary, (Do I have to give my age?) It's 41
Satellite Engineer
Mt. Airy, Maryland

Peanut Butter and Onions Sandwich

2 thick slices of red onion
1 tablespoon of sweet butter
4 slices of whole grain bread
gourmet chunky peanut butter

Sauté onion slices in sweet butter until slightly brown. Place on 2 bread slices.
Spread peanut butter on other slices and cover onions. Enjoy!

Serves 2

Matt Nieporent, age 15
Son of Tracy Nieporent, Director of Marketing of Montrachet
New York, New York

BT&P

My favorite peanut butter sandwich doesn't call for jelly. You toast some bread,
spread with peanut butter, and then add bacon and tomatoes. Ummmm

Lori, age 44
Chef/Homeschooling mother of two
Phoenixville, Pennsylvania

Peanut Butter & Jelly on Rye with Bacon and Caramelized Onions

1 medium onion, sliced thin
2 tablespoons vegetable oil
4 slices rye bread, lightly toasted
8 slices bacon, fried crisp
4 tablespoons crunchy peanut butter
2 tablespoons grape jelly

Sauté onions in vegetable oil over medium high heat until golden brown. Set aside. Spread a thin layer of peanut butter on all 4 slices of bread. Top 2 slices of bread with 4 slices of bacon on each and caramelized onions. Spread grape jelly on remaining slices of bread and place on top to create the sandwich. Cut in half or quarters and serve with your favorite BBQ potato chips.

Makes 2 sandwiches

Matthew Franklin, age 36
Chef/Owner, 240 Union Restaurant
Lakewood, Colorado

Toasted Peanut Butter & Bacon

Toast 2 slices of white bread. Butter one side of each slice with softened butter. Slather peanut butter onto buttered slices. Layer on at least 3 slices of cooked bacon. Sandwich peanut butter sides together. Chew. Yum Yummmm.

Susan Regis, age 39
Chef, Biba
Boston, Massachusetts

Bagel Ham & Jelly

I take a bagel and (skip the peanut butter . . . yuck) lay a piece of ham on it. Then glop jelly onto the ham, put the top on, and enjoy! I normally use a raisin bagel with apple jelly. Yum! The ham is the best part.

Oh, I occasionally spread a tad of peanut butter on it.

Joanna Lynn, age 12
San Angelo, Texas

PB&J&O

2 slices whole grain bread
peanut butter
raspberry jam
green Spanish olives (say about 7 of them)
carrot

Put peanut butter on one slice of bread and raspberry jam on the other. Set the olives on the peanut butter bread at equal distances apart from each other. Cut a carrot into really thick slices and lay 3 or 4 slices on the jam bread. Then gently, carefully merge the 2 pieces of bread into one sustainable and manageable, delicious treat. Best eaten with Fritos and a Coke or juice or milk. YUMMMMMMMMYYYYYYY!!!!!!!!!!!!!

Steve, age 44
President, WordHampton Public Relations
East Hampton, New York

Peanut Butter Pita

Adding sprouts and carrots to your peanut butter sandwich adds crunch. Putting it all in a pita makes it fun to eat.

1 tablespoon peanut butter
1 teaspoon mayonnaise
2 tablespoons shredded carrots
1 teaspoon raisins
1/2 large or 1 small pita pocket
2 tablespoons alfalfa sprouts

Combine peanut butter with mayonnaise. Add carrots and raisins. Stuff mixture into pita pocket. Top with alfalfa sprouts.

Serves 1

Sandra K. Nissenberg MS, RD, and Barbara N. Pearl, MS, RD
Authors of *Brown Bag Success*
Buffalo Grove, Illinois

Meeker Family
Peanut Butter Sandwich

This is a family favorite that goes back to Kevin's grandfather and now is enjoyed by his three children. The secret to a good peanut butter sandwich? There has to be enough peanut butter that it sticks to the roof of your mouth.

6 slices whole wheat bread
3 heaping tablespoons creamy or crunchy peanut butter
3 tablespoons sweet relish
3 tablespoons mayonnaise

Toast the bread, then spread 3 slices liberally with peanut butter. Spread the sweet relish on top of the peanut butter. Spread the mayonnaise on the other 3 slices and place on top of the peanut butter ones. (Be sure to put mayo on the dry slice, otherwise you'll end up with a dry sandwich.) Cut sandwiches in half and serve with mesquite flavored potato chips.

Makes 3 sandwiches

Kevin Meeker, age 48, daughter Leigh, age 10, and sons Connor and Nolan, ages 5
Chef/Owner, Philadelphia Fish & Company
Philadelphia, Pennsylvania

Peanut Butter and Cheese Melt

1 slice wheat bread
1 tablespoon peanut butter
1 slice American cheese

Spread the peanut butter on the bread. Place the cheese on top of the peanut butter. Put it in the microwave and heat until the cheese melts, about 10 to15 seconds. Cut the bread into 4 squares.

Jordan, age 8
Featured in *I Made It Myself*
by Sandra Nissenberg, MS, RD, and Heather Nissenberg
Buffalo Grove, Illinois

Peanut Butter Nachos

nacho chips
refried beans
peanut butter
guacamole
salsa

Spread nacho chips on a baking tray. Top with refried beans and peanut butter. Heat in oven until beans are warm and peanut butter is melted. Remove from oven and top with guacamole and salsa. Serve hot.

Roy, age 14
Ocean City, New Jersey

Peanut Butter and Jelly "Sushi" Style

2 ½ cup servings cooked sticky rice
2 tablespoons sesame paste
2 tablespoons red bean paste

Press cooked sticky rice into flat pad. Spread with sesame paste; then with bean paste. Roll jelly-roll style and slice into rounds.

Tracy Nieporent, age 49
Director of Marketing, Nobu
New York, New York

Main Meals
and Side Dishes

Pictured left: Joe Brown of Melange Cafe and his son Jordan.

Peanut Butter and Jelly Quesadillas

8 8-inch flour tortillas
8 tablespoons peanut butter
4 tablespoons strawberry jelly or preserves
2 tablespoons sugar
4 tablespoons sour cream
1 pint strawberries, washed and stems removed
juice of 1 lime

Take 4 of the flour tortillas and spread each with 2 tablespoons of peanut butter. Spread jelly on remaining tortillas. Lay tortilla flat, jelly side up, and top with peanut butter tortilla, peanut butter side down.

Spray a nonstick fry pan with coating spray and warm pan over medium heat. Place a quesadilla in the pan and brown on each side. Repeat process with each quesadilla. (Hold them in a warm oven while you finish the recipe.)

In a small bowl, whisk together 1 tablespoon of sugar with sour cream; set aside. Slice strawberries and toss with lime juice and remaining sugar. Remove quesadillas from oven and cut each one into 4 pieces. Divide among 4 plates. Top with a dollop of sour cream and strawberries in center of each plate.   Serves 4

Trish Morrissey, age 28
Executive Chef, Philadelphia Fish & Company
Philadelphia, Pennsylvania

Peanut Butter Pasta

1/4 pound pasta rings, cooked and cooled
8 ounces ricotta cheese
1/2 cup dark raisins
1/4 cup sliced almonds
1/2 cup grape jelly
2 tablespoons water
1/2 cup creamy peanut butter

Mix the cooked pasta with the ricotta cheese, raisins, and almonds. In a small saucepan, add the jelly and water, stir in the peanut butter, and heat until warm. Drizzle heated peanut butter sauce over top of individual pasta servings.

Serves 4 to 6

Francis Anthony, the "Love Chef"
Author of *Cooking Pasta with Love*
New York, New York

PB&J Pasta

I like my PB&J made with linguine, spinach, artichokes, pine nuts, and a light olive oil and garlic sauce. Yum! A big salad is nice to go with it, and a good chianti wine perfects the evening. Put a little 1950's vintage Johnny Cash on the stereo, and the scene is set for redneck romance! Hooga wooga!

Quentin, age 32
Engineer
Norman, Oklahoma

Ham in Peanut Sauce

1 slice ham, 1/2-inch thick
1 teaspoon prepared mustard
1/3 cup peanut butter
4 tablespoons brown sugar
4 medium-sized ripe bananas

Preheat oven to 350°. Put ham in flat casserole or baking dish. Spread on mustard and peanut butter and sprinkle with 2 tablespoons brown sugar. Bake for 30 minutes. Arrange peeled bananas around ham, sprinkle with remaining brown sugar, and bake 10 minutes longer.

Serves 4

This was my mom's "secret" recipe which I was able to finally pry out of her.

Bob, age 28
Third Grade Teacher
Washington, D.C.

West African Chicken with Peanut Flavors

1 3-pound whole chicken, cut into 1/8 pieces
salt and ground white pepper
3 ounces olive oil
1 cup diced onions
1 cup diced leeks, whites only
1 cup diced celery
1/4 cup thinly sliced blanched garlic
3 cups peeled plum tomatoes and their juice
1 teaspoon curry powder
1 teaspoon cumin
1 teaspoon turmeric
1/2 teaspoon coriander seed
2 cups chicken broth
1 tablespoon harissa or sambal or Chinese chili paste
1/2 cup whole shelled roasted peanuts
1/2 cup creamy peanut butter

Wash and dry the chicken segments. Season liberally with salt and pepper. Heat the olive oil in a large marmite or stew pot. Once the oil is very hot, add the chicken pieces and brown them evenly on all sides. Remove the chicken and add the vegetables. Sauté a few minutes and add all the spices. Mix well and continue cooking for 2 minutes. Add the liquids and bring to a boil. Add the harrisa or sambal or chili paste, peanuts, and peanut butter. Reduce to a simmer. Cover and cook over very low heat on top of the stove for 45 minutes. Remove the cover, bring back to a simmer, and cook another 15 minutes. Stir occasionally so bottom doesn't scorch. Serve with steamed rice and harrisa.

Jonathan Eismann, age 37
Chef/Owner, Pacific Time and PT Cafe
Miami, Florida

Peanut Butter and Pork Sate

2 pounds boneless pork shoulder or loin, cubed
1/2 Spanish onion, cut into large 1-inch pieces
1/2 cup chunky peanut butter
1 tablespoon sesame oil
2 red chiles, chopped
1 tablespoon sesame seeds
1 tablespoon light soy sauce
1 tablespoon lime juice
salt and fresh ground pepper
Summer Lettuce Salad with Jelly Vinaigrette (see recipe)

Thread pork and onion onto skewers. Thoroughly combine remaining ingredients and brush lightly onto the pork brochettes. Let brochettes rest 1 to 2 hours in the refrigerator.

Bring them back to room temperature before grilling. Grill on medium heat, brushing often, until cooked through but still moist. Serve over Summer Lettuce Salad with Jelly Vinaigrette.

Michael P. Foley
Chef/Proprietor, Printer's Row
Chicago, Illinois

Summer Lettuce Salad
with Jelly Vinaigrette

2 tablespoons grape jelly
2 tablespoons rice wine vinegar
squeeze of 1 lime
1 clove garlic, smashed and worked into a paste
1/2 cup extra virgin olive oil
4 cups summer salad greens of your choice
salt and pepper to season

Mix the grape jelly, wine vinegar, and lime juice with the garlic paste. Slowly stream in the olive oil. Place half of it in large bowl. Add the mixed greens and toss gently. Season with salt and pepper. Add more dressing to taste.

To plate, place greens on 4 plates. Top with pork brochettes.

Michael P. Foley
Chef/Proprietor, Printer's Row
Chicago, Illinois

Peanut Butter Cabbage Rolls

When I was a young lad growing up in Pennsylvania, like most youngsters, I was enrolled in summer camp. (Camp Sequanota in Jennerstown, PA... if anyone cares.) Besides learning about nature and such, we were usually treated to different foods. One of these was Peanut Butter Cabbage Rolls. Now being the youngster that I was, I would've probably eaten anything, but I have on occasion recreated this combination of tastes with great remembrances to a time long gone.

Very simply, take one leaf of RAW cabbage (do not use red cabbage, I'm not fond of the color combination); spread moderately with peanut butter; and roll. (If anything, this may be a way to get your young ones to eat greens.)

Rino, age 36
Systems Administrator, Jet Propulsion Laboratory
Pasadena, California

Peanut Butter and Jelly Potatoes

medium-sized sweet potatoes
milk
salt and pepper to season
peanut butter
jelly

Scrub and bake potatoes in a moderate oven (375°) for 45 minutes. Scoop out the centers. Mash with milk and season with salt and pepper. Refill potato skin halfway. Put in a tablespoon each of peanut butter and jelly. Fill with remaining mashed potatoes. Return to oven for 15 minutes.

Randy, 33
Physician
Canton, Ohio

Sweet
Sandwiches

Sundae Sandwich

potato bread
peanut butter
gummi bears
Sour Patch Kids
mini marshmallows
chocolate fudge
caramel syrup
chocolate crunchies (like the kind in the middle of ice cream cake)

Spread peanut butter on top of potato bread. Stick gummi bears and Sour Patch Kids in the peanut butter. Top with marshmallows and some chocolate fudge. Cover with another piece of potato bread. Cover the outside of the sandwich with caramel sauce and then coat it with crunchies.

This sandwich is sticky, and sometimes it gets soggy, so you might want to eat it with a fork and knife.

Jennifer, age 9
Ocean City, New Jersey

As seen on The Tonight Show with Jay Leno!

The 21 Decker

21 slices of bread
peanut butter
strawberry jelly
peanuts
Butterfinger pieces
candy coated peanut butter pieces
1 piece of string licorice
3 candy coated chocolate pieces

Take a piece of bread and put peanut butter and jelly on it. Add peanuts and sprinkle crushed Butterfinger and candy coated peanut butter pieces on it. Do that 19 more times and top with last slice of bread. Put licorice on top for a mouth, 2 candy coated chocolate pieces for eyes, and 1 for a nose.

Hallie, age 10
Mt. Laurel, New Jersey

FINALIST! The Kid's Ultimate Peanut Butter and Jelly Contest.

As seen on The Tonight Show with Jay Leno!

Chocolate Covered Peanut Butter and Jelly Sandwich

2 slices white bread
1 tablespoon of your favorite peanut butter
1 tablespoon black raspberry jam
4 ounces dark chocolate

Make a sandwich, spreading first the peanut butter and then the jam. Press the edges of the sandwich firmly together to close. Place the sandwich in the freezer for about 10 minutes.

Melt the chocolate in a double boiler. Take the sandwich out of the freezer and place it on a wire rack. Pour half of the chocolate on top to cover the bread and return the sandwich to the freezer for 2 minutes. Flip the sandwich over and cover the other side with chocolate. Place in refrigerator for 2 minutes before eating.

Olivier De Saint Martin, age 36
Chef/Owner, Dock Street Brewery & Restaurant
Philadelphia, Pennsylvania

Glutteny Crusade Sandwich

1 to 12 chocolate iced chocolate doughnuts
1 clown horn (to toot your excitement)
1 spoon (Don't stick it on your nose.)
1 jar of your favorite peanut butter
1 clown nose (to smell the goodness)
1 knife (plastic for you youngsters!)
1 giant glass of milk

This is a very delicate process so you must be careful. The first step is to stick your head into the doughnut box and devour all doughnuts but one. (Toot! Toot!)

Take the remaining doughnut and slice lengthwise like a bagel. Take the spoon off your nose and use it to scoop out the middle of the bottom portion of the doughnut. Open peanut butter (Oooh, smell peanutty goodness!) and use the knife to generously spread it into the empty space in the lower half of the doughnut. Lick your fingers clean and put the top of the doughnut back on the lower half. Count to three and dig in! Don't forget the milk! Toot! Toot!

Shlo Bo Bean Boy™
Clown, Friend to All
All over the USA, but mostly in Alaska

Toasted Puffed Mallows

peanut butter
marshmallows
chocolate syrup

Put the peanut butter on the bottom slice of toast. Place marshmallows on top and cover with chocolate syrup, then the top piece of toast. Nuke it for about 30 seconds until the marshmallows blow up like big balloons. Let sit for a second until the sandwich shrinks back down to size.

Ron, age 28
Jupiter, Florida

Chocolate Doughnut Sandwich

Cut a chocolate doughnut in half. Eat 1 piece and put butter on the other one. Then put on peanut butter. Let your mom cut up an apple. Put apples on top.

Christopher, age 3
Philadelphia, Pennsylvania

Peanut Butter and Jello

2 plain or chocolate doughnuts
1/2 cup of your favorite red jello
peanut butter
one can of instant whipped cream
one bowl of cherries

Slice donuts in half. Place jello on 1 donut half. Spread some peanut butter on the other half. Combine halves and top with a small amount of whipped cream. Place cherries on top of whipped cream.

Serves 2

Robby, age 11
Son of Tracy Nieporent, Director of Marketing of Tribeca Bakery
New York, New York

Madeleine & Isaac's Pinwheel Chubby

2 long slices of white bread cut length-wise from an unsliced loaf of bread
smooth peanut butter
marshmallow spread at room temperature
strawberry jam
1 bag of candy coated chocolate pieces

Roll the bread with a rolling pin so it is very thin. Spread a thin layer of peanut butter across the bread, leaving a strip (about the width of 2 of Madeleine's fingers) uncovered. Carefully spread the marshmallow over the peanut butter, leaving another strip (about the width of 2 of Isaac's fingers) with no marshmallow, only peanut butter. Spread the jam over the marshmallow even with edge of the marshmallow/peanut border. Sprinkle the candy over the whole sandwich but not too close together.

   Carefully roll the sandwich up, holding it lengthwise so the sandwich is really chubby. (Spread the clean edge of the bread with some peanut butter. This will hold the roll closed once it is rolled.) Seal the buttered end and cover with a cloth. Place it in the refrigerator so it firms up, about 15 minutes.

Wayne Gibson, age 33, son Isaac, age 4, and daughter Madeleine, age 6
Executive Chef, Castle Hill Inn and Restaurant
Newport, Rhode Island

Peanut Butter Cup Sandwich

2 pieces of white bread
1/2 of a chocolate candy bar
peanut butter

Toast the bread. On first piece, put the candy bar half. On second piece, smear peanut butter. Put slices of bread together. Enjoy!

Katie, age 13
Daughter of Jim Coleman, Executive Chef of Treetops in The Rittenhouse
Moorestown, New Jersey

PB&J
Desserts

Pictured left: Don Pintabona of Tribeca Grill and his daughter Daniela.

Hazelnut-Peanut Butter and Strawberry Fritters

1 cup peanut butter
1/2 cup hazelnut butter
1/2 cup strawberry jam
1 cup flour
1 teaspoon baking powder
coarse salt to taste
1 extra large egg
1 cup good quality beer
1 pint strawberries, sliced
1/2 cup sugar
vegetable oil for frying
whipped cream

Gently fold the butters and jam together. Roll into walnut size balls and chill 3 to 4 hours or overnight.

Using a whisk, combine flour, baking powder, salt, egg, and beer thoroughly. Let the batter rest for 15 minutes. Mix strawberries and sugar together and set aside.

Line a baking sheet with paper towels and set it next to the stove. In a frying pan, heat 1 inch of vegetable oil over moderate heat. One at a time, dip the peanut butter pieces in batter and lay them in hot oil. Don't crowd them in the pan. Leave room for all pieces to cook evenly. Regulate the heat to be sure the batter doesn't burn. It should take 7 to 8 minutes for the fritters to turn golden brown and very crisp. Drain well on paper towel and serve immediately with marinated strawberries and whipped cream.

Waldy Malouf, age 44, and daughter Merrill, age 12
Executive Chef, The Rainbow Room
New York, New York

Peanut Butter Mousse in a Phyllo Cup with Melba Sauce

1/3 cup heavy cream
1/2 cup granulated sugar
1 cup creamy peanut butter
3/4 cup heavy cream, loosely whipped to soft peaks
Phyllo Cups (see page 88)
Melba sauce (see recipe)
crushed peanuts (optional)

Place the 1/3 cup cream and granulated sugar in a saucepan over high heat and bring to a boil. As soon as the mixture boils, remove it from the heat immediately. Add the peanut butter and gently whisk until the mixture is smooth. Allow the mixture to cool and thicken, about 1 hour.

Once the peanut butter mixture has cooled, gently fold in the remaining whipped cream, taking care not to deflate the cream. Place the mixture into a piping bag with a large star tip and pipe it into the prepared phyllo cups. (The mousse can be scooped with a large spoon if no bag is used.) Place the mousse cups in the refrigerator until serving time.

When ready to serve, drizzle the melba sauce from the end of a spoon in a zigzag pattern across the base of 4 dessert plates. (A pastry bag with a fine tip also can be used.) Place a mousse cup on each plate; then drizzle more sauce over the mousse, if desired. Sprinkle the top of the mousse with crushed peanuts, if desired.

Melba Sauce

1/2 cup water
1/2 cup granulated sugar
1 cup red raspberry preserves

Place the water and granulated sugar in a small saucepan and bring to a boil, allowing the sugar to dissolve. Add the preserves and bring the mixture back to a boil, stirring constantly for 1 minute. Remove the mixture from the heat and strain immediately through a fine-meshed strainer or through cheesecloth to remove the seeds. (If seedless preserves can be found, omit this step!) Allow the sauce to cool and thicken.

Meridith Ford, age 37
Food Writer and Chef Instructor, Johnson & Wales University
Norfolk, Massachusetts

Phyllo Cups

4 to 5 frozen phyllo sheets *
3 tablespoons butter, melted

Preheat the oven to 400°. After the dough has thawed to room temperature, lay the phyllo sheets flat. Measure the dough into 5x5-inch squares, keeping the dough covered with a slightly moistened paper towel. With a sharp knife, cut through the layers of dough where the squares are marked. Gently fold scraps and extra sheets, wrap them, and place them back in the freezer for later use.

To make the cups, spray a muffin tin with a nonstick coating or brush with butter. Working quickly so that the dough does not dry out, place 1 phyllo square at the bottom of 4 of the muffin molds. Place a drop of melted butter in the center of each phyllo square. Place another square on top of each bottom square, rotating the square three-quarters to the right. Repeat the process of squares and butter so that each phyllo cup has 5 squares of phyllo fanned out to form a cup. Bake the "cups" in the oven for 8 to 10 minutes, or until golden brown. Remove the cups and set aside for later.

Meridith Ford, age 37
Food Writer and Chef Instructor, Johnson & Wales University
Norfolk, Massachusetts

Peanut Butter and Jelly Fold Up

3 tablespoons cream cheese
3 teaspoons sugar
3 tablespoons peanut butter
3 tablespoons jelly
1 box puff pastry
powdered sugar

Preheat oven to 350°. Mix cream cheese and sugar until smooth. Add peanut butter and jelly. Blend until creamy. Use puff pastry according to directions. Spread pastry on the baking sheet; then spread mixture on top of pastry. Fold lengthwise and bake for 15 minutes. Cool and sprinkle powdered sugar on top and serve with a cold glass of milk.

Justin, age 14
Oaklyn, New Jersey

Peanut Butter and Almond Strudel with Strawberry Glaze

6 phyllo dough sheets

1 cup melted butter

2 cups peanut butter

1 cup sliced almonds, toasted

1½ cup coconut, toasted

1 cup marshmallow spread

1 8-oz. jar strawberry preserves

1 pint fresh strawberries, cleaned and cut in half.

Follow thawing instructions on phyllo pastry box.

When ready to assemble strudel, preheat oven to 350°. On working surface place enough parchment paper, foil, or plastic wrap to border phyllo dough. One sheet at a time, butter phyllo dough with pastry brush, placing another sheet of dough on top. Continue until all 6 sheets have been buttered.

Spread peanut butter on phyllo dough. Take toasted almonds and coconut and sprinkle on peanut butter. Spread marshmallow spread on almonds and coconut.

To roll strudel, grab corners of parchment paper, foil, or plastic base, lift, and fold several times until all dough is rolled. Brush strudel with melted butter and bake until golden and crisp to your satisfaction.

In medium saucepan, heat preserves until slightly warmed. To serve, slice two 1-inch pieces of very warm strudel and put them on a serving plate. Drizzle with glaze. Place 2 strawberries on top.

Note: Fun for kids but can be messy. Use caution, peanut butter will be hot.

Dan Dogan, age 33, and James Austin, age 33
Executive Chef and Sous Chef, Terrace at Greenhill
Wilmington, Delaware

Peanut Butter and Jelly Ravioli

1 cup flour
1 tablespoon hazelnut spread
1 egg
1/3 cup peanut butter
1/3 cup ground almonds
2 tablespoons blueberry jam
1/2 cup fudge

Mix the flour and hazelnut spread with a little bit of water. Add egg and mix until a ball of moist dough forms. Refrigerate for 1 hour.

On a floured surface, roll out dough, relatively thin, and cut into four 6-inch rounds. Combine the peanut butter and almonds. In the middle of 2 circles, spread some peanut butter paste, then jam, and cover with remaining peanut butter paste. Cover with remaining dough circles and press down on all sides to seal. Dampen edges (about 1/8-inch from the edge) with water.

Cook giant raviolis in boiling water until the dough is tender. Drain and serve with hot fudge.

Olivier De Saint Martin, age 36
Chef/Owner, Dock Street Brewery & Restaurant
Philadelphia, Pennsylvania

Peanut Butter Topping

your favorite ice cream – vanilla and chocolate are good choices
peanut butter

Put your ice cream into a bowl, but leave room for some dollops of peanut butter. Mix lightly and eat.

Charles, age 85
Stockbroker
Cincinnati, Ohio

Sort of a S'more

My favorite peanut butter recipe is softened vanilla ice cream blended with creamy peanut butter and spread on chocolate graham crackers!!
Happiness-Peace-Love!

Meliss, age 16
Omaha, Nebraska

Elvis' Twist

This dessert, featuring his favorite foods — chocolate and peanuts —creates a taste that would have made Elvis twist and turn. Good eating, hail to Elvis.

cake-style brownie mix and required mix ingredients
2 bananas
semi-sweet chocolate chips
crushed peanuts
vanilla ice cream
peanut butter
raspberry jam
chocolate sauce, fresh raspberries, peanuts, and whipped cream for garnish

Bake brownie mix according to directions on the box and allow to cool. While brownies are baking, slice bananas into 3 long strips. Melt chips, dip bananas in melted chocolate, and sprinkle them with crushed peanuts. Place on a cookie sheet covered with wax paper. Freeze for at least 30 minutes.

When brownies are suitable for cutting, slice in 3x3-inch squares; then slice through the middle to produce thin squares. Using a 3-inch ring mold (or a clean tuna can with the ends cut out), cut pieces of vanilla ice cream out of the carton, making each round 2 inches thick.

To serve, spread peanut butter on one piece of the brownie square and raspberry jam on the other. Place an ice cream round on the jam, the frozen banana slice next, and top with the peanut butter covered brownie. Place the sandwich on a plate and garnish with chocolate sauce, raspberries, peanuts, and whipped cream.

Serves 6

Colin T. Ambrose, age 39
Chef/Owner, Estia
East Hampton, New York

Chocolate Waffle with Peanut Butter Cream and Jelly Beans

2 waffles
4 ounces chocolate, melted
2 tablespoons strawberry jam
4 ounces peanut butter
1/3 cup whipped cream
1 small bag of jelly beans

Brush the waffles with the melted chocolate and let it cool. When the chocolate is solid, place some jam in each of the waffle holes.

Mix the peanut butter with the cream and pipe it on the waffle in a zigzag design with a pastry bag. Add the jelly beans —use them to write "me" and "you."

Lauren, age 8
Daughter of Olivier De Saint Martin, Chef/Owner of Dock Street Restaurant
Cherry Hill, New Jersey

Peanut Butter Waffle Sandwich

2 eggs, separated
1½ cups flour (2 parts white, 1 part wheat)
3 teaspoons baking powder
1/4 teaspoon salt
2 tablespoons sugar
1 cup milk
2 tablespoons shortening
4 cups peanut butter
2 cups raspberry jam
4 cups ice cream
1/2 cup powdered sugar

Beat the egg whites until fluffy; set aside. In another bowl, mix egg yolks, flour, baking powder, salt, sugar, milk, shortening, and 2 cups peanut butter. Fold in egg whites. Cook waffles according to waffle iron instructions. Let cool. Top half the waffles with the remaining peanut butter; then jam and ice cream. Smash each top with another waffle to make a sandwich. Dust with powdered sugar and serve.

Joe Brown, age 37, and Jordan, age 3
Chef/Owner, Melange Cafe
Cherry Hill, New Jersey

Peanut Butter Pizza

1 cup warm water
1/2 tablespoon yeast
3 tablespoons maple syrup
3 cups unbleached white flour
1/4 cup peanut flour
1/2 teaspoon sea salt
2 tablespoons peanut oil
1/2 cup coarsely chopped freshly roasted Virginia peanuts (shelled)
1/2 cup creamy organic peanut butter (I like Arrowhead Mills)
1/4 cup finely chopped dried organic figs
1/4 cup fresh ricotta cheese
2 navel oranges, peeled and very thinly sliced
2 Golden Delicious apples, cored and thinly sliced
2 Bosc pears, cored and wafer sliced
1/2 cup organic raisins
4 tablespoons turbinado sugar
1/2 teaspoon cinnamon

Warm water enough so finger can be inserted without pain or blister. Stir in 1 tablespoon maple syrup and then add yeast. Allow to bubble, saying the magic words "Hubba Bubba, Hubba Bubba." Place both flours and salt in mixing bowl and tumble through your fingies. Add 1 tablespoon of peanut oil and do same. Begin to add yeast/water mixture, smooshing between fingers and palms. Continue until completely blended, adding more flour if needed to make the wad slightly tacky, as in "tacky pizza," but not sticky.

Chuck (as in "blend in") in the ground peanuts and squeeze throughout the blob of dough. Take 1 tablespoon of peanut oil and coat a large bowl. Place dough blob inside, coating it too. Cover with plastic wrap and allow to rise for about 50 minutes in 100° oven or in a warm window. Crush down, squeezing out all the bubblies, and spread on a round pizza baking tray. Blend peanut butter with crushed figs. Preheat oven to 400°.

With a spatula, coat the entire surface with the peanut butter/fig spread. Ditto with ricotta. Distribute the orange slices on top. Do the same with the apple and pear slices. Sprinkle the raisins, making a perfectly random pattern, envisioning each bite containing about 2.3 raisins. Take the remaining tablespoon of maple syrup and perform a drip painting, again thinking of each bite. Mix sugar and cinnamon and sprinkle in a glitter tossing motion over entire top.

Place pizza in oven for 10 minutes. Reduce heat to 350° and continue to cook another 20 minutes until toast-smelling and crispy on the edges, and nearby spectators begin to salivate. Remove. Allow to settle and continue to salivate for 3 to 4 minutes and then serve it up.

Peanutbutter™, age 49
Visual Artist
Philadelphia, Pennsylvania

Peanut Butter and Jelly Pizza

2 sheets frozen puff pastry, thawed
1/3 cup creamy peanut butter
1/3 cup cream cheese
1 tablespoon milk
1 teaspoon sugar
1/2 cup strawberry fruit spread, jam, or jelly
3 to 4 ounces white chocolate, grated
2 whole strawberries

Preheat oven to 375°. Using a sharp pastry knife, cut a 9-inch circle from each sheet of puff pastry. (Use a cake or pie pan as a guide.)

Put peanut butter and cream cheese in a microwave safe bowl. Microwave on HIGH for 25 seconds. Remove from microwave and stir to combine.

Place a piece of parchment paper on baking sheet OR spray baking sheet with vegetable oil spray. Put 1 of the pastry circles on baking sheet. Spread peanut butter and cream cheese mixture on the pastry circle. Make sure to leave a 1/2-inch border around the edge. Put the other pastry circle on top of the peanut butter mixture. Pinch the edges of the 2 circles together to seal. Crimp the edge to make a rim to hold in your "pizza sauce."

Use a pastry brush to brush milk all over the top and sides of the pastry.

Sprinkle sugar evenly over the whole "crust." Put the baking sheet in the oven and bake for 15 minutes.

Using a sharp knife, cut thin slices from the sides of the strawberries, leaving the inside of the berries in the shape of a square. (Each berry should give you 4 "pepperoni-like" slices.) Remove the crust from the oven and spread strawberry jam over the top of the crust. Return pizza to hot oven and bake for 5 to 7 more minutes. Remove from the oven and sprinkle with grated white chocolate. Arrange strawberry "pepperoni" on top of the chocolate and allow the pizza to rest until the chocolate is melted. Slice pizza into 8 wedges and serve while warm.

Riki Senn, age 30-something, and Cindy McCutcheon, age 20-something
Director and Coordinator, The Greenbrier's Cooking School
White Sulphur Springs, West Virginia

Gooey and Chewy Pizza

1 premade pizza shell
peanut butter
bananas, thinly sliced (you decide how many)
superfine sugar
honey coated peanuts
marshmallow spread

Preheat oven to 400°. Prebake pizza for 1 to 1½ minutes. Scoop out inside of pizza, leaving rim and a thin bottom intact. Spread with desired amount of peanut butter and top with bananas. Sprinkle with superfine sugar and bake until crunchy, about 30 minutes. Remove from oven and sprinkle with honey coated peanuts. Squiggle marshmallow spread all over. Eat it before anyone else does!!!!

Don Pintabona, age 38, and son Alex, age 3
Executive Chef, Tribeca Grill
New York, New York

Peanut Butter Marshmallow Brownie

5 tablespoons butter
1 ounce unsweetened chocolate
2 eggs
dash vanilla
3/4 cup flour
3/4 cup brown sugar
1/3 cup marshmallow spread
2/3 cup chunky peanut butter

Preheat oven to 350°. Melt butter and chocolate together over low heat. Set aside until lukewarm. Beat the eggs with the vanilla. Stir in flour and sugar. Stir in butter and chocolate mixture. In a separate bowl, beat marshmallow and peanut butter until smooth.

   Grease 9-inch square baking pan. Pour in batter and swirl in peanut butter mixture. Bake 25 to 35 minutes.

Daniel, age 14
Son of Albie Buehrer, Owner of Indian Rock Produce
Quakertown, Pennsylvania

Peanut Butter & Jelly Streusel Bars

1/2 cup shortening

1¼ cups firmly packed brown sugar

3/4 cup creamy peanut butter

3 tablespoon milk

1 tablespoon vanilla

1 egg

1¼ cups all-purpose flour

3/4 teaspoon baking soda

3/4 teaspoon salt

1 cup strawberry jam (or your favorite jam or jelly), stirred

1/2 cup quick oats, uncooked

Preheat oven to 350°. Grease 13 x 9-inch baking pan. Combine shortening, brown sugar, peanut butter, milk, and vanilla in large bowl. Using an electric mixer, beat at medium speed until well blended. Add egg. Beat just until blended. Combine flour, baking soda, and salt. Add to creamed mixture at low speed. Mix just until blended.

Pat 2/3 of dough in bottom of prepared baking pan in an even layer. Spread jam evenly over crust to within 1/4 inch of sides. Combine remaining dough with oats. Dough will be somewhat stiff. Drop by spoonfuls onto jam layer. Press lightly to even out dough layer. Bake 20 to 25 minutes or until edges and streusel topping are lightly browned. Cool completely on wire rack. Cut into bars.

Peanut Butter & Jelly Fondue

Make a peanut butter sauce for dipping by blending or hand mixing peanut butter, honey, and water to dipping consistency. Melt any type of jam or jelly and soak bread or pound cake cubes in it. Place cooled cubes on skewers and dip into peanut butter sauce. Sauce may be served either hot or cold.

Michael McNally, age 42, and son Jake, age 8
Chef/Owner, London Grill
Philadelphia, Pennsylvania

Jam Squares

Jam Squares are a teatime favorite at The Queen Victoria. Any flavor jam may be used, but the innkeepers have found they like raspberry or strawberry best.

3 cups flour
1 cup sugar
1 teaspoon baking powder
1 teaspoon cinnamon
1/2 teaspoon cloves
1 cup butter or margarine, softened
2 eggs, beaten
1 teaspoon vanilla
raspberry or strawberry jam

Preheat oven to 350°. Sift dry ingredients together. Cream butter; then add eggs and vanilla and mix well. Add dry ingredients. Spread half mixture in a greased 10x15-inch cookie sheet. Spread generously with jam. Crumble remaining dough over jam. Bake for 45 minutes or until lightly browned.

Joan and Dane Wells and their daughter Elizabeth, age 15 1/2
Innkeepers, The Queen Victoria® Bed & Breakfast Inn
Cape May, New Jersey

Gramma Lewis' Peanut Butter Fudge

2½ cups sugar
1 stick butter
1 can canned milk
6 ounces chococolate chips
1 6-ounce jar marshmallow spread
1 teaspoon vanilla
3 tablespoons peanut butter
1 cup chopped nuts

Boil sugar, butter, and milk for 6 minutes, stirring constantly. Remove from heat and add chocolate chips, marshmallow, vanilla, peanut butter, and nuts. Beat until it thickens. Place in greased dish. Cool and cut into squares.

Breakfast
a la PB&J

French Toast with Roasted Bananas

4 pieces of raisin bread
2 tablespoons peanut butter
1 tablespoon raspberry jelly
1 egg
1 cup milk
1 drop vanilla extract
2 ounces butter
1 banana cut in half
2 vanilla ice cream balls

Make 2 sandwiches with the bread, peanut butter, and jelly. Press edges down firmly. Beat the egg and milk with the vanilla and pour into a deep plate or shallow bowl. In a nonstick pan, heat 1 ounce of butter until bubbling. Dip sandwich in batter; then pan sear the bread on both sides. Serve hot.

In another pan, heat the other ounce of butter. Roast the banana in the hot butter and let cook until it caramelizes. Place on top of the French toast. Top each sandwich with one ball of ice cream.

Lauren, age 8
Daughter of Olivier De Saint Martin, Chef/Owner of Dock Street Restaurant
Cherry Hill, New Jersey

Fried PBJ

10 slices white bread
peanut butter to taste
jelly to taste
2 eggs, beaten
1 tablespoon flour
1 cup evaporated milk
1 teaspoon sugar
1 teaspoon salt
oil for frying

Spread peanut butter and jelly on white bread. Set aside. Combine eggs, flour, milk, sugar, and salt. Preheat oil in skillet. Dip sandwich in batter. Dip quick — don't let it sit in batter!

Fry in oil until golden brown . . . ahhh French toast and PB&J all together. Sprinkle with powdered sugar if you like.

Batter coats 5 sandwiches

Dawnelle Lee, age 49
Chef/Owner, Cafe Sarah and Creative Catering
Kokomo, Indiana

Ooh La La PB&B

croissant
butter
1/2 banana, sliced
brown sugar
peanut butter
heavy cream, whipped

Slice croissant in half. Spread with butter; top with banana and brown sugar. Broil until sugar starts to bubble. Immediately spread on peanut butter. Top with whipped cream.

Kelly Reardigan, age 30
Paralegal and Author of the soon-to-be-released
The Junk Food Goddess Speaks
Collingswood, New Jersey

PB&J Double Decker Crepe

1 egg
1/2 cup flour
1 cup milk
1 teaspoon butter, melted
3 ounces chocolate chips
1 cup whipped cream
2 tablespoons chunky peanut butter
2 tablespoons raspberry jelly

Mix egg into flour; then slowly whisk in milk. Add 1/2 teaspoon of the melted butter. Let sit for 20 minutes.

Rub some of the butter into a nonstick pan. Make 5 crepes (1/8-inch thick), cooking each on both sides. Allow crepes to cool slightly.

Mix chocolate chips into whipped cream. Spread 1 tablespoon peanut butter on the first crepe. Layer on another crepe and spread on 1 tablespoon jelly. Repeat. Top with a crepe. Using a spatula, cover the whole cake with the whipped cream. Cut into 4 quarters and serve.

Olivier De Saint Martin, age 36
Chef/Owner, Dock Street Brewery & Restaurant
Philadelphia, Pennsylvania

Sam & Kevin's MacNut Peanut Butter Breakfast Sandwich

Sam Choy and Kevin Meeker travel together, cooking to raise money for Big Brothers Big Sisters. This recipe is one they came up with during those travels.

1/4 cup finely chopped unsalted macadamia nuts
1/4 cup finely chopped unseasoned bread crumbs
1/2 teaspoon cinnamon
1/2 teaspoon five-spice powder or clove
2 whole eggs, beaten
4 tablespoons milk
4 tablespoons creamy peanut butter
8 slices bread — your favorite is fine
Tropical Fruit Salsa (see page 116)
4 tablespoons butter
1 can nonstick cooking spray

Place the macadamia nuts in a blender and chop fine. (This can be done by hand using a knife or putting the nuts in a bag and smashing with a heavy object — like your shoe.) In a bowl, mix the macadamia nuts, bread crumbs, cinnamon, and five-spice powder. Set aside.

In a shallow bowl, beat the eggs and milk; set aside. Spread the peanut butter on 4 of the slices of bread and place a tablespoon of the tropical fruit salsa on top of the peanut butter and spread evenly. Top with the remaining slices of bread.

Spray a nonstick skillet with nonstick cooking spray and heat skillet over medium high heat. When hot, remove from stove, add 1 tablespoon of butter, and return to heat.

Take one of the sandwiches and gently dip into egg-milk mixture; turn sandwich over and dip other side. Each piece of bread should be wet but not soaked or bread will fall apart. Gently place sandwich into bread crumb mixture and cover on both sides. Place sandwich in hot skillet and cook until light, golden brown. Turn sandwich and do the same to other side. Repeat for the other 3 sandwiches, using 1 tablespoon of butter per sandwich for cooking.

To serve, place a large scoop of tropical fruit salsa onto the center of a plate. Cut the sandwich into quarters and place around salsa. Serve immediately for breakfast or dessert.

Serves 4

Sam Choy and Kevin Meeker
Sam is Chef/Owner of 5 restaurants in Hawaii and Tokyo and host of "Cooking with Sam Choy" in Hawaii
Kevin is Chef/Owner of Philadelphia Fish & Company and 2 other restaurants in Philadelphia and has appeared on "Ready ... Set ... Cook!"

Tropical Fruit Salsa

2 large ripe bananas, peeled and diced
2 large ripe mangoes, peeled and diced
2 whole ripe papaya, peeled and diced
1 whole orange, juice only
1 teaspoon minced fresh ginger root
2 tablespoons sugar

Place the diced fruits into a large mixing bowl. Stir and mix together. Reserve 4 tablespoons of the fruit for the sandwiches. To the remaining fruit, add the orange juice, ginger, and sugar. Mix until sugar is dissolved.

Sam Choy and Kevin Meeker
Sam is Chef/Owner of 5 restaurants in Hawaii and Tokyo and host of "Cooking with Sam Choy" in Hawaii
Kevin is Chef/Owner of Philadelphia Fish & Company and 2 other restaurants in Philadelphia and has appeared on "Ready . . . Set . . . Cook!"

Peanut Butter Spreadin' Dipity

Peanut butter supplies protein, but also more than enough fat. I've designed this recipe to minimize the fat while maximizing the protein absorption. For your body to use the protein that is provided by peanut butter, it needs to be eaten with complementary proteins such as those from whole grain breads. Enjoy!

1/2 cup Strained Yogurt (see recipe)
1/2 cup creamy peanut butter
1 banana, peeled and mashed

In a small bowl, combined the strained yogurt, peanut butter, and mashed banana. Enjoy 1 tablespoon of this spread on a slice of whole wheat bread, muffin, or even a waffle!

Graham Kerr, age 64
International Culinary Consultant
Camano Island, Washington

Strained Yogurt

Put 1½ cups plain nonfat yogurt (no gelatin added) in a strainer over a bowl or use a coffee filter, piece of muslin, or a paper towel and place it in a small sieve over a bowl. Cover and let it drain in the refrigerator for 12 hours or overnight. There is about a 25% volume loss. Yields 3/4 cup.

Peanut Butter & Jelly Muffins

2 cups whole wheat flour
1/2 cup sugar
1½ teaspoon baking powder
1/2 teaspoon salt
3/4 cup crunchy peanut butter
3/4 cup skim milk
2 small eggs
1/4 cup fruit preserves

Preheat oven to 375°. Combine the flour, sugar, baking powder, and salt in a mixing bowl. Cut in the peanut butter with two forks or a pastry blender until the mixture resembles coarse crumbs. Add the milk and eggs all at once, stirring until the flour is moistened.

Place 2 tablespoons of the batter into a greased fluted or plain muffin cup. Place 1 teaspoon of the preserves in the center of the batter and top with 2 tablespoons more of the batter. Repeat until you have 12 muffins. Bake for 15 to 17 minutes. Remove from the muffin cups and cool on a rack.

Serves 4

Greaves Surprise Buns

It is normally made with leftover bread dough but could easily be made with frozen dough.

bread or sweet dough enough for 1 loaf (frozen dough can be substituted)
2 cups peanut butter
2 bananas, sliced into 1-inch thick rounds
2 cups Greaves or your favorite jam (strawberry, raspberry, tripleberry, etc.)

Roll out the dough into a square 3/4-inch thick. On half of the dough generously spread peanut butter. Place banana slices on the peanut butter side approximately 2 inches apart. On the other side of the dough spread your favorite jam. Fold jam side over peanut butter/banana side.

With a glass or cookie cutter, cut out circles, keeping the banana slices in the center. Place buns onto a greased baking sheet and let rise for 2 hours. Bake in a preheated 350° oven for approximately 20 to 25 minutes. Enjoy!

Angela, age 32
Vice President, Greaves Jams & Marmalades Ltd.
Niagara-on-the-Lake, Ontario, Canada
www.greavesjams.com

Peanut Butter and Jelly Bread

2 cups all-purpose flour
1/2 cup sugar
1 teaspoon baking powder
1 teaspoon salt
3/4 cup peanut butter
1 egg, slightly beaten
1 cup milk
1/4 cup strawberry or raspberry preserves

Preheat the oven to 350°. In a large bowl, combine the flour, sugar, baking powder, and salt. Cut in the peanut butter with an electric beater on medium speed until well combined. Add the egg and milk; stir until well blended.

Spread half the batter into a 9x5-inch loaf pan that has been coated with nonstick cooking spray. Spoon the preserves down the center of the batter. Top with the remaining batter, covering the preserves completely. Bake for 55 to 60 minutes or until a wooden toothpick inserted in the center comes out clean. Invert onto a wire rack and let cool completely. Slice and serve.

Mr. Food
Cookbook Author and Syndicated TV Chef

Reprinted with permission from HELP MR. FOOD®! COMPANY'S COMING!, William Morrow, Inc., 1995.

Breakfast Apple Surprise

2 slices of bread
creamy peanut butter
1 small apple, washed
1 tablespoon raisins

Spread peanut butter on bread. Slice apple into thin wedges and place evenly on 1 peanut buttered bread. Sprinkle raisins over the other peanut buttered bread. Place both pieces of bread together, with the apples and raisins facing each other, and cut into 4 pieces. I like to eat this on Saturday mornings. I hope you enjoy this as much as I do.

Barbara, age 8
Merchantville, New Jersey

INDEX

Participating Restaurants

240 Union Restaurant, Lakewood, Colorado
Biba, Boston, Massachusetts
Cafe Sarah and Creative Catering, Kokomo, Indiana
Castle Hill Inn and Restaurant, Newport, Rhode Island
Dock Street Brewery & Restaurant, Philadelphia, Pennsylvania
Estia, East Hampton, New York
Hana-Maui Hotel, Maui, Hawaii
London Grill, Philadelphia, Pennsylvania
Melange Cafe, Cherry Hill, New Jersey
Montrachet, New York, New York
Nobu, New York, New York
Pacific Time and PT Cafe, Miami, Florida
Philadelphia Fish & Company, Philadelphia, Pennsylvania
Printer's Row, Chicago, Illinois
Stein Eriksen Lodge, Park City, Utah
Terrace at Greenhill, Wilmington, Delaware
The Greenbrier, White Sulphur Springs, West Virginia
The Herbfarm, Fall City, Washington
The Manele Bay Hotel, Lanai, Hawaii
The Queen Victoria® Bed & Breakfast Inn, Cape May, New Jersey
The Rainbow Room, New York, New York
The Rittenhouse, Philadelphia, Pennsylvania
Tribeca Bakery, New York, New York
Tribeca Grill, New York, New York
Tutor and Spunk's Deli, Dana Point, California

Participating Authors/Celebrities

Francis Anthony, the "Love Chef" · Lauren Chattman · Sam Choy ·
Edward Feldman, Star of the Learning Channel's "Furniture To Go" · Mr. Food · Graham Kerr ·
Heather Nissenberg · Sandra K. Nissenberg MS, RD · Barbara N. Pearl, MS, RD · Kelly Reardigan

?

Do you have a favorite PB&J recipe?

Admit it . . . all this talk of peanut butter and jelly has made you hungry. We're hungry too — for more recipes! Send us your favorite PB&J recipe (sandwich, dessert, breakfast, etc.) and we may include it in our next book.

My PB&J Recipe

Recipe Title _____

Ingredients/Instructions _____

_____

_____

_____

You may submit recipe on another piece of paper, but it must be accompanied by this signed release form. Please mail to Small Potatoes Press, 1106 Stokes Avenue, Collingswood, NJ 08108.

❏ I agree to have the submitted recipe included in Small Potatoes Press publications. I understand that there will be no financial remuneration or compensation for such inclusion (other than publicity), and I will seek none. I will not hold the publisher liable for any errors or typographical mistakes. Small Potatoes Press has the right to restrict the inclusion of any recipe.

Printed name/Signature _____ Age _____

Occupation/Title _____ Phone _____

Address/City/State/Zip _____

PB&J USA Mail Order Form

Please send the following:

- ❏ _____ copies of *PB&J USA* - $10.95
- ❏ _____ copies of *Local Flavor: Favorite Recipes of Philadelphia Area Chefs* - $15.95
- ❏ _____ copies of *Jersey Flavor: Favorite Recipes of Garden State Chefs* - $15.95
  (to be published November 1998)

Sales Tax: *PB&J USA:* NJ addresses please add $.66 (6%)
Local Flavor: NJ addresses please add $.96 (6%)
Jersey Flavor: NJ addresses please add $.96 (6%)

Shipping: $3.00 for the first book; $1.00 for each additional book

Payment: Please make your check or money order payable to:

Small Potatoes Press
1106 Stokes Avenue, Collingswood, NJ 08108
609-869-5207

SHIP TO: _____

_____

❏ Is this a gift? If so, please include your name and full address.

_____

_____

Thank you!